— IN THE PRESENCE OF —
GARY PLAYER

A PERSPECTIVE ON THE LIFE AND PHILOSOPHY
OF ONE OF THE WORLD'S GREATEST GOLFERS

Forrest Beaumont

THIS BOOK WAS MADE POSSIBLE BY THE GENEROUS SUPPORT
OF THE FOLLOWING SPONSORS

SIGMA

2

A portion of the proceeds

from the sale of this book

will be donated to the

Gary Player Foundation

for underprivileged children's

education around the world

Foreword

This book tells a story – a very brief glimpse into the daily life of one of the greatest sportsmen the world has known – Gary Player. The story is relayed to us by means of a collection of beautifully executed photographs by Forrest Beaumont. This dedicated and highly-skilled young photographer has set out to create this archive and I think he has achieved his goal superbly. There have been other books written about Gary Player but this collection of photographs and words will remain a true and accurate archive for the future beholders of "The Gallery of Great Men".

As a professional golfer, Gary Player spent most of his career beyond the shores of our country, South Africa. He was always perceived as being one stage removed from the harsh world of politics. Yet few men in our country's history did as much to enable those in power to see the light and, thus, enact political change that improved the lives of millions.

Gary Player has achieved, through his influence as a great athlete and human being, what many politicians have not. He did it with the courage, perseverance, patience, pride, understanding and dignity that would be extraordinary even for a world leader.

During those many years I spent in prison, I was frequently aware of the inappropriately harsh treatment that Gary Player had to endure by virtue of the fact that he represented a country whose people were generally condemned at the time for their support of 'apartheid'. Many attempts at disrupting his play were evidenced by millions of viewers worldwide. On one occasion, Jack Nicklaus, the greatest golfer of all, intervened with the help of his golf club in an effort to restrain a rush of demonstrators. Given all this, Gary Player still succeeded in achieving second place in this Major PGA Championship – perhaps his finest ever performance – notwithstanding the demonstrators' attempts to put him off!

There were many other instances around the world where politically motivated demonstrations were directed at Gary Player in an attempt to disturb his play. Even the American FBI acted as his 'protectors' – and, through all this, he remained composed, endured all that was thrown at him and stood his ground. Most admirable, I think!

Gary Player also succeeded in persuading the Government at the time, to allow golfer, Lee Elder and tennis player, Arthur Ash, to compete on South African soil. Furthermore, he established the 'Gary Player Foundation', of which I am proud to serve as a Patron. This foundation is doing an enormous amount to further the education of young, underprivileged people and partners, with my own Nelson Mandela Children's Fund, in staging the annual Nelson Mandela Invitational pro-celebrity golf events.

I will always remember, on my release from prison, saying to Gary Player: "You have not received the recognition you deserve". My words were most sincere.

Gary Player was voted Sportsman of the Century in South Africa and his accomplishments as a golfer are extraordinary. He won 163 tournaments worldwide, which compares most favourably with the greatest golfers of all time. Over five decades, he achieved the highest accolades, including the Grand Slam of golf. He was also voted one of the top five most influential people in our nation's history. His accomplishments as a humanitarian and statesman are equal to, and may even surpass, his accomplishments as an athlete. His legacy will last forever and Forrest Beaumont's wonderful book, so ably published by Umdaus Press, will always be a reminder and a 'living archive' of a great man, my friend, Gary Player.

Nelson Mandela

Acknowledgements

The world consists of many truly remarkable individuals of whom I am fortunate to know a few. This book would not have come into being had it not been for their generous support and guidance. I am thankful to my parents for their undying support and for introducing me to photography at an early age. My father's photographic work has always inspired me; my mother's loving support encouraged me during the challenging times. High on my list of those who have played a significant role in my life, are my beloved grandfather, my mentor, Dimitri Karalis and long-time friend, Johan Marais. They have proven to me through their own successes that ambition can, by steadfast pursuit of a dream, become reality.

My sincere appreciation goes to the following persons for their kind assistance and advice: Marc Player, Beatrix Geen, Stella Helwick, Stephen Katzef, Gary Shap, Beverly Vorster, Max Fowles, Wayne Fowles, Gida Campbell, Pam Campbell, Debbie Longenecker, Eric Dunn, Ronell Buitenbos and Steve Lewis.

For their continuous support I owe a debt of gratitude to the following companies: Black Knight International, Sigma, Acer, SanDisk, Budget Rent a Car and ExecuJet.

To Tersia van Rensen, for spending many a late night committing her incredible design skills to the creation of a special and unique book, thank you Tersia, I appreciate it dearly. Sincere thanks to Steve Bales, Lourens du Plessis and Simon Jooste for generously contributing their skills to the compilation of this book.

For having touched my heart in extraordinary ways, I would like to acknowledge the following friends and loved-ones: Lee Hung-Wei, Lourens du Plessis, Ruan Strydom, Simon Jooste, Lilo Müller, Motoko Reinle, Shizuko Ouwehand, Steve Bales, Helen & Lemmer du Plessis, Aretha Strydom, Adri & Leon Miller, Cameel Makhoul, Troy Constandakis, Tony & Nanette Rogerson, Victor Bortot, Derek & Lerie Brink, Raymond & Evelyn Clarke and Charles de Ravel.

Finally, to Gary and Vivienne Player, and the Player family: thank you for your generous hospitality and for the invitation into your lives, through which this book was made possible.

Forrest Beaumont

Introduction

The art of photography has experienced many changes in its almost two hundred years of existence. Its ability to capture detail has improved. Its capacity for conveying atmosphere has increased. With the advent of motion pictures in the twentieth century, the future of still photography may have been in peril; yet its widespread use has only increased. The reason may be similar to that of lovers in daily contact with one another who still write love letters. The joy of captured expression lies in a prolonged and unhurried experience of the medium. This is why lovers opt to impart some little essence of themselves to the surface of a page and why such a letter once received is read and re-read, and then read once again. The medium of photography has the same ability to capture some of the spirit of its subject. It is why one may experience the extraordinary feeling when viewing a photograph, that life itself is holding its breath; that time has stopped to capture the moment forever.

The creation of *In the Presence of Gary Player* has afforded me the undiluted pleasure of spending time with a legend. It has given me the opportunity to encapsulate moments of truth and beauty. In a way, the mere company of Gary Player challenged and motivated me; the fact that I could see for myself how the determined will of this man kept him competitive in professional golf for more than fifty years.

Accompanying the photographs, are a collection of principles and rules of thumb, frequently quoted by Gary Player. Though some have emerged from the public conscience, and are well known by all, most have had their origin in the mind and life of the great man himself. Both by the time I spent with him, and by this wisdom of years that he has penned for publication, I have gained a glimpse into his mindscape that has left me with the firm conviction that Gary Player is not only an ambassador of sport, business and charity work, but a true ambassador of life.

Gary Player

Born in South Africa in 1935 to Harry and Muriel Player, Gary was the youngest of three children. At age eight, he lost his mother to cancer; an event that, coupled with his father's working long hours in the gold mines of Johannesburg, brought on a solitary childhood.

Player's passion for golf began at the age of fourteen when he played his first round. He parred the first three holes and was hooked for life. He then met Jock Verwey, a professional who would become instrumental in teaching the young Player the fundamentals of golf. He also became acquainted with Jock's daughter, Vivienne, whom he would later marry.

In 1953 Player turned professional, embarking on a career that would span more than five decades. His achievements include winning nine Major Championships consisting of three Masters, three British Opens, two PGA Championships and the US Open as well as nine Senior Major Championships consisting of three Senior PGA Championships, two Senior US Opens, three Senior British Opens and the Senior Players Championship.

Well known for staging some the most spectacular and memorable comebacks in the game's history, and for his trademark black clothing, Player was aptly dubbed the 'Black Knight'. His dedication to fitness and his world-wide promotion of golf has earned him the titles: 'Mr. Fitness' and 'the International Ambassador of golf'.

Along with Golf-greats, Gene Sarazen, Ben Hogan, Jack Nicklaus and Tiger Woods, Player is one of only five players to have won golf's Grand Slam. This feat ensures his status as one of the most successful golfers of all time. To date Player has won 163 championships worldwide and has travelled nearly fourteen million miles. He is the World's Most Travelled Athlete™.

Player is a distinguished golf course architect with over 200 courses throughout the world attributed to him. Black Knight International, owned and operated by his son Marc Player, includes Gary Player Course Design and Gary Player Enterprises. It also manages the Gary Player Foundation that has as its primary objective, the promotion of education for underprivileged children.

In 2003 Player, a member of the Laureus World Sports Academy, received their coveted Lifetime Achievement Award in Monte Carlo.

Other than golf, his interests include the breeding of thoroughbred race horses, for which the Gary Player Stud Farm has received world-wide acclaim.

He enjoys spending time with his six children and more than a dozen grandchildren.

Player was recently named South Africa's Sportsman of the Century and one of the five most influential people in the history of his country.

Many people would have you believe that we live in a world of ever-increasing complexity and that the demands on our time make it nearly impossible to focus on doing any one thing well. The truth is that we impose this idea upon ourselves. Life, and golf as a reflection of it, remains simple if you can only manage to keep an unclouded view of where it is you are going.

We fail to arrive at our goals when we allow ourselves to be distracted from looking at them from an unobstructed point of view. We humans are remarkable in our ability to invent distractions. The purpose in striving is to get the thing done, not to worry about how you get the thing done.

There is an interesting consequence to the idea that winning can only come through determination and hard work. There are some who would suggest that to win at anything – to make the big sale, win the big case, make the big putt – one must be blessed with a little bit of luck at precisely the right moment in time.

Goose Valley, Eastern Cape, South Africa

THE HOLE IN ONE

The hole in one: The beauty of a truly remarkable shot brings the realisation that sometimes good things happen for reasons that we cannot fathom. This very feeling is part of the wonder of life. Since we cannot make everything happen in life, sometimes we just have to try our best, and let happen what will.

My travels have taught me that, until you exhaust your study of a subject, you never fully comprehend it. If you don't fully comprehend something, you cannot get the maximum amount of joy out of it.

The World's Most Travelled Athlete™

It's not what you have,
it's what you do with
what you have that
makes all the difference.

Gary's garden at Blair Atholl, Johannesburg, South Africa

Absence is to love what wind is to fire;

it extinguishes the small and kindles the great.

With wife, Vivienne Player

*The day you lose the ability to tell your children you love them –
no matter how old they are – is the day you've lost something
you cannot replace.*

Lunch with daughter, Theresa

Spending time with grandson, William

THE
LESSON

CURIOSITY:

The key to learning about anything in life
is to be curious about everything.

Every morning when you rise, there are choices you can make.

You can choose to be happy or sad, positive or negative, productive

or idle, fit or unfit. I think it is important to recognise, first of all,

that there are such choices and then, of course, to choose wisely.

CHOICE

The three most cherished possessions I have
are my family, my faith and my health.

THERE IS NO SUCH THING AS DUMB LUCK

There are dumb people who presume, at some point, that something lucky will happen. Determined people presume that nothing will happen unless they make it happen.

I will say without hesitation that you cannot achieve any goal if you have negative thoughts. You must have positive and, what might seem to others, bold thoughts.

35

I firmly believe that the way we think determines what we are and what we can be. We create our success or failure primarily by our thoughts.

I strongly believe that the ability to accept adversity and overcome it is one of the most important virtues because it offers us the greatest opportunities for growth.

As more and more changes enter my life,
I have vowed to accept them for what
they truly are: opportunities.

If I had to give just one definition of a good golfer it would be: the man who has the determination to win and the patience to wait for the breaks.

HE HARDER YOU PRACTISE,
THE LUCKIER YOU GET

Chatting with Leonard Thomas

There is no substitute for personal contact.

I am convinced that the routine of personal discipline I have observed since boyhood, has been the real reason I have endured as a champion and as a competitor. It has taken various forms, not least of which is the physical fitness routine I follow every day. There is, however, a value more important than the feeling of well-being that this ritual brings, it is the complete control and mental discipline to follow these punishing exercises, even when the body screams, 'stop!'

You only get one opportunity
to make a first impression.

In life it is important for us to remember that our fellow competitors are not our enemies. There are many stories about how, during World War I, the troops from both sides would cease hostility during Christmas-time, and, in some cases, even get together and sing in shared moments of humanity. These were men who were literally trying to kill each other and yet they were still able to look out across No-Man's-Land and realise that on the other side there was a group of men in the same situation.

Gary with Charl Schwartzel at the Nelson Mandela Invitational

Every round of golf we play teaches us

the importance of having a goal and also

having a logical plan to achieve that goal.

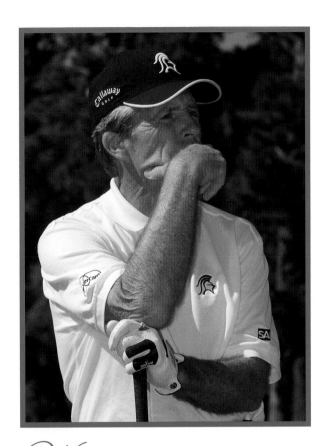

We have to plot the way before we begin the advance towards our goal.

I don't wear black as a superstition; I wear it because it is my trademark.

Some players wear certain colours superstitiously and for me that is bad.

Many people are superstitious about the number thirteen. I don't believe

in that kind of nonsense. If I did it could really upset me very much indeed.

There is an old saying in golf regarding the inability to perform when we over-analyze a situation: "Paralysis by analysis." This condition occurs when we lose sight of the single goal of golf – to hole the ball in as few strokes as possible – and instead become wrapped up in the idea of "how" we do each aspect of the game.

Perfection is no little thing, but little things make perfection.

PERFECTION

Always making time for his fans. Signing anything from shirts to hats…

IT IS PEOPLE THAT MATTER MOST, NOT THINGS.

The game of golf provides us with a never-ending stream of challenges to our honour and dignity. The insights these challenges offer into our own souls provide us with an invaluable commodity; the ability to look at ourselves in the mirror and know that we are honourable people.

HONOUR

The true value of sportsmanship does not lie solely in the fact that it is always an admirable idea to take the high road. As you well know by now, I think winning is important – very important. Importantly though, winning is not the only thing of significance.

Bobby Skinstad, South Africa's former Springbok rugby captain and Gary

Enjoy the success of others just as ___ would want them to enjoy yours.

My years in golf have taught me a fundamental truth. Life is enriched by passionate pursuits. In my mind, the best passions are those that last a whole lifetime.

PASSION

As I travel regularly from country to country, I've come to know many of the world leaders in business, politics and sports. Upon close examination, all of them seem to share one common trait: the will to overcome the adversities of life and turn them into success… the determination to win in spite of the reverses and handicaps that in one way or another come to all of us

Date
Datum 16|11|2003
or Bearer
of Toonder

Mandela Children's Fund

A PERSON'S LIFE GRAPH cannot reflect "ups" all the time;

every person is bound to have some "downs". But the person who has a positive
mental outlook... who visualises good things happening... who expects the best,
doesn't stay down very long. Perspective is regained rapidly and things begin
to work out.

To keep your mind open to learn new things
is to keep progressing forward in life.

The Blair Atholl School for underprivileged children, developed and supported by the Gary Player Foundation

The opportunity to make a difference in the lives of others does not thrust itself upon us. Importantly though, we do not need to look hard for it either. So when you spot the chance to give back to the world, act on it. You will have made life better for others and for yourself.

75

We who play the game know that sometimes we get pleasant and unexpected surprises, such as a hole-in-one or a ball that skips off the water and on to dry land. We also know that we are equally likely to get a bad break – a wild bounce of the ball, a sudden gust of wind. The game leaves us no choice but to accept the good with the bad and to move on to the next shot. In other words: we take what the game deals us, and we do the best we can to move forward. This is the way life is, and the grand old game of golf will never let you forget it.

We all seek the keys to success, but success does not look for us. We must pursue it. When the pursuit is fuelled by determination and hard work, things fall into place with remarkable ease.

The opening ceremony of the Presidents Cup, 2003, at Fancourt, South Africa.
Jack Nicklaus, Former US President George Bush, South African President Thabo Mbeki and Gary Player.

Our sorrows will far outnumber the joys, but the joys will far outweigh the sorrows.

Greeting Jaime Patiño from Valderama

Your mind is just like your body: the more you exercise it, the better it works. There is only one way to exercise your mind: use it. The only way to use it is to constantly feed it with new information. If you open your eyes, they will open your mind to new things. Once you start, it will be just like physical exercise: the more dedicated you are to learning, the more you will learn.

Concentration takes years of practise to acquire. It is difficult to come by and easy to lose if you let up. An integral part of developing concentration is self-discipline: the kind of self-control that teaches your mind to do what you want it to do.

Analysing the next hole
with Adam Scott

Meters

With Ernie Els

It's not the size of a man in a fight: it's the size of the fight in a man.

Player and Nicklaus – rivals, competitors, friends

Press interview with Jack Nicklaus at the Presidents Cup, 2003

FRIEND

SHIP

Friendship is special and of the greatest importance in life.

Developing the art of thinking positively is the best way I know to handle those times when everything may not be going just right.

THINKING
POSITIVELY

Sharing thoughts with Presidents Cup teammate K.J. Choi

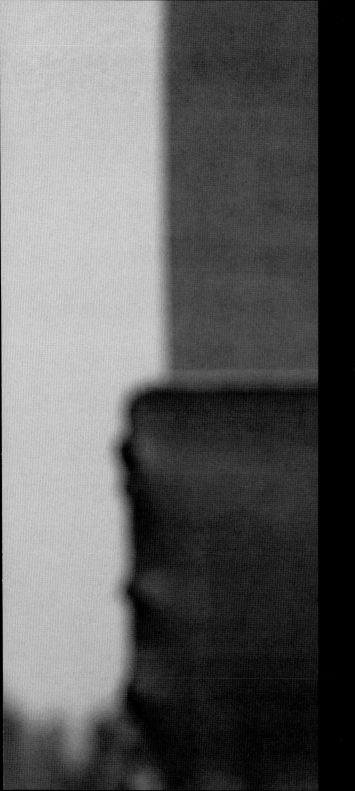

very triumph in life is a complete test of skill and character. In order to win a championship or a personal victory, you must subject yourself to the oddest of torments. As the pressure builds in any situation, it is normal to yearn for escape. This is fear in its most simple form: the feeling that things would be made much easier by avoiding the challenge that is about to transpire. The torment lies in the tug of war between your instincts, which say, "Run!" and your spirit, which says, "Stand fast and fight."

Granddaughter Antonia, Gary and wife, Vivienne

It is vitally important in life that we pursue our goals with the clearest of minds. By regularly making certain that the lines of communication are open along every channel, I have been able to pursue my competitive dreams without the constant nagging feeling that I might somehow be leaving a family member in the lurch.

*T*o be true to ourselves,

we must be true to others.

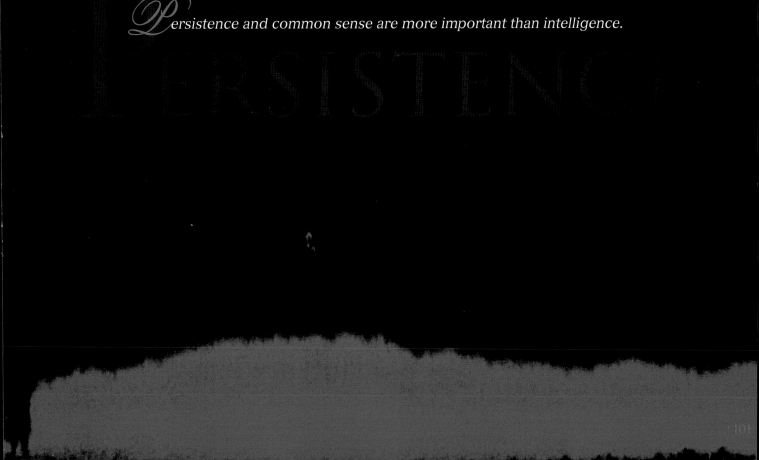

Persistence and common sense are more important than intelligence.

PERSISTENCE

If you seek success in any form, you are obliged to make your best effort in the face of adversity. The secret to achieving this best effort is clarity of thought and focus. Achieve this, and you will execute.

CLARITY OF THOUGHT AND FOCUS

Giving former US President George Bush putting tips – Presidents Cup, 2003

We have all benefited from those who came before us: our parents, our teachers, and those who long ago took the same path that we aspire to. To acknowledge them in your mind is to understand that no one gets where he is going without the help of others. Your instinct should tell you that just as they helped you, you must help others.

The corollary between the game of golf and the pursuit of excellence in the rest of our lives is, to me, an obvious one. The opportunities to achieve our goals are so rare that, when they present themselves, we must give the fullest effort of which we are capable.

REST
IS
RUST

When you consider how difficult it is to win at golf, it becomes quite apparent that anything less than a total commitment to winning means that you will probably never come out on top. The same can be said for all pursuits.

Roger Maltbie and Gary Player

In the afterglow of victory, the best-remembered moments are those when the fear was acknowledged and put to rest.

When I use the word 'determination' I suppose
I mean that one simply never gives up.

There is no success without effort. There is no reward without work. Some people think life owes them something: wealth, respect or peace of mind. I don't mind telling you that this attitude makes me sick.

Player entertaining

Staying fit requires time, dedication and focus. Because it is such a challenge, fitness makes demands on our minds as well as our bodies. This in turn strengthens us mentally.

Player's daily exercise regimen

We are all born with some amount of determination. Often though, we need more than what comes naturally to us. The additional determination we need to excel must be cultivated from within. After all these years, I have no doubt that this process of cultivatio. begins with the discipline of keeping our bodies in shape.

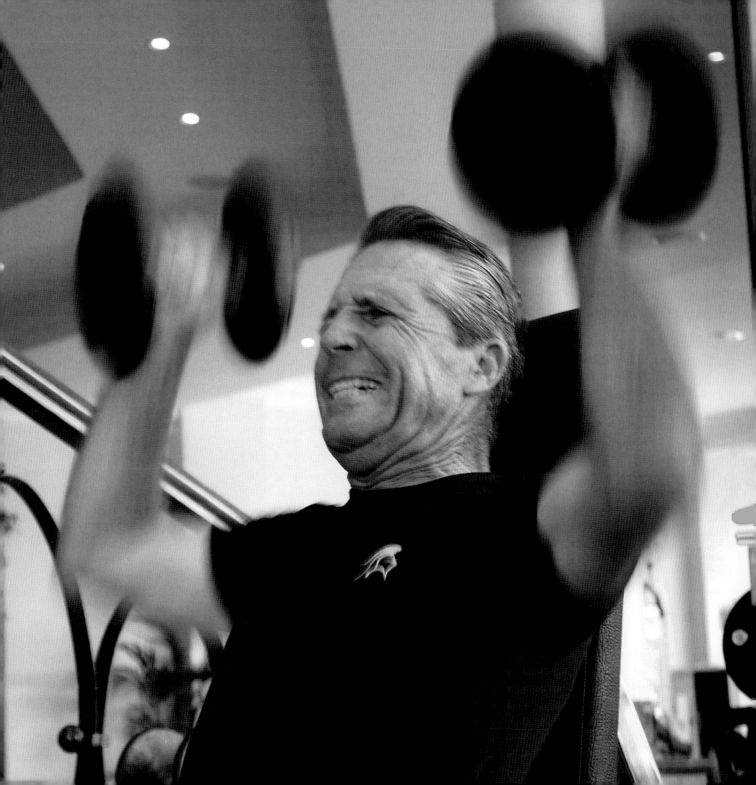

Experience has taught me that going through a full workout at times that I do not feel like it, does more than just tune my body. It also feeds the fierce self-discipline I need to sustain me when I am under pressure in tournaments.

Everything in business is negotiable except quality.

Son Marc, Gary and wife Vivienne viewing development plans

Accept the advice of the man who loves you, though you like it not at present.

ADVICE

Son Marc and Gary

You have to "see" your goals
happening in your mind's
eye for them to become a reality.

THE PATH TO FULFILMENT

Doers realise that any goal of substance is not meant to be achieved easily and that they will face severe tests of their patience and determination along the path to fulfilment.

Gary Player – the greatest bunker player of all time

PREPARATION

PRECEDES

PERFORMANCE

I like to remember the words of General Douglas MacArthur, who said, "You build courage, when courage seems to fail. You regain faith when there is little cause for faith, and create hope when hope is lost. Learn to laugh, never forget to cry. Be serious, but don't take yourself seriously."

It is not the difficulties we encounter but how we deal with them.

Don't be a fool. Do not just pass time on this earth: live your life. The sorriest man is the man who knows he gave up before he exhausted his efforts because he must look back and wonder, "What if?"

Whenever I am wearing my golf shoes and I walk across a paved surface, I am some-how reassured by the crunching noise I hear. It is the audio version of comfort food. When I hear the crunch, I know I am in the right place, among the right people, doing something I love.

It seems to me that great champions have little in common save a love for the game and the dedication to it that permits them to work endlessly to perfect their talents. This ability to fight is really more the hallmark of a champion than any technical excellence in the swing.

*If you want to do something badly enough,
have the patience to realise that minor
setbacks on the road to the end are just that
– minor.*

Even now I can still recall the mixture of exhilaration and fear as I clambered on a horse for the first time in my life; feeling the great animal begin to break from a walk into a canter and then into a gallop. I was nine years old.

THERE IS SOMETING
ABOUT THE OUTSIDE
OF A HORSE THAT IS
GOOD FOR THE
INSIDE OF A MAN

REVELATIONS

Embracing the revelations that are brought to us by curiosity serves to enrich our lives.

Gary on his stud farm in the Colesberg District

A positive approach applies to everything you do. You can fill your mind with good thoughts or abuse it with bad ones. You can put your faith in God or worry needlessly. You can work at your marriage and family life or you can neglect them. You can set high goals and be productive or drift through life, never achieving what you might (and should) have done, considering your gifts. I think that the key to a happy and productive life is having multiple goals.

WHAT IF

If you stay determined to live life fully, you will never become a "what if" man, you'll be surprised by the source of motivation that suddenly appears to you.

I am inclined to be impatient. I have enthusiasms. I like to get things done. When I am on the farm, I often wear a pair of heavy ankle boots which have lots of straps and laces. They are a little hard to arrange and I often find myself in the truck and driving off from the house with the whole thing undone and my boots not properly tightened up. I am in such a hurry to get to where I am going. This is a small battle that I have to fight, and I have to fight it in golf too.

PATIENCE

The fear of change is really the fear of the unknown. Man knows no greater fear than that of the unknown. It always strikes me as odd that people get consumed by this fear of change because, when you think about it, every-day we're alive is unknown to us before we live it.

For all we take in life we must pay.

We are all capable of doing great things when we acknowledge that we have never achieved all there is to do in our lives.

The world is filled with what I refer to as dreamers and doers. Dreamers don't do anything to achieve their goals, whereas doers are dreamers with a difference – those who are willing to make the necessary sacrifices to achieve success.

FEAR OF THE UNKNOWN

Go ahead if you like. Not me.

To fear it is never to know the wonder of new-found things.

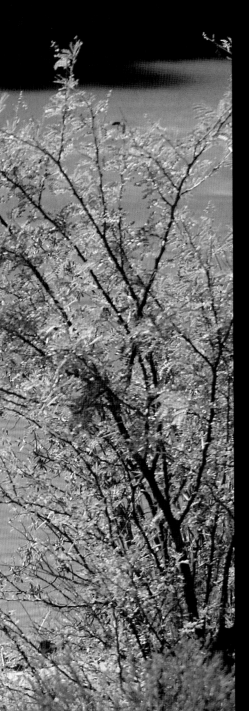

The pride that can be derived from knowing that someone considers you a mentor is beyond quantifying. The impact of your efforts may very well be the beginning of a string of events in that person's life that may otherwise never have occurred.

Skipping stones on the river with grandson Joseph

It is only with the heart that one can see rightly;
what is essential is invisible to the eye.

Grandsons James and Joseph trying to remove a splinter

In all probability, the best contribution any man can make is by his example. If now or at some time in the future, somebody draws strength from this personal story of the lonely, undersized boy from South Africa who refused to accept the odds, both on and off the fairways, and triumphed against them, then my purpose has been served. It was all worthwhile. There will remain some memory that I had striven to be the best; that I refused to settle for less.

With grandson Joseph

If you keep the character-istics of youth – a forward-looking, strong mind in a supple, strong body – your chronological age won't matter. You'll be productive as long as the good Lord wills it and no one can ask for more than that.

With granddaughter Savannah

Player enjoying the holidays with his family

physically fit person can do everything better, thinking, working, playing, sleeping, reading – everything.

'Tending the garden' with grandson, William

WE ARE CREATURES OF EMOTION

With grandson Damian

ONCE I OPENED MY MIND TO NEW THINGS,

I realised that I must keep it open; I must look upon life as a continual learning process. Those who fail to realise this, remain stuck in the same place their entire lives.

The intellectual and emotional rewards of exploring life are waiting for you around the corner and across the seas.

GO AND GET THEM...

UMDAUS PRESS
P.O. BOX 11059
HATFIELD
0028
SOUTH AFRICA

E-mail: umdaus@succulents.net
Web site: www.succulents.net

FIRST PUBLISHED 2004

Text© Gary Player

Photographs© Forrest Beaumont

DESIGN Tersia van Rensen & Forrest Beaumont

PRODUCTION Alex Fick & Kotie Retief

EDITING Liz Fick

PRINTING Tien Wah Press, Singapore

SPECIAL BINDING Peter Carstens

ISBN 1-919766-28-5 (Sponsors edition)
ISBN 1-919766-29-4 (Standard edition)